EARLY CHRISTIAN IVORIES

EARLY CHRISTIAN IVORIES

by

JOSEPH NATANSON

1953

ALEC TIRANTI LTD.

72 CHARLOTTE STREET

LONDON, W.1

Made and printed in the United Kingdom

FOREWORD

THE writer wishes to express his special thanks to Mr. H. D. Molesworth, Dr. G. Zarnecki and Mr. P. Lasko in London, to Prof. C. Cecchelli in Rome, to Prof. C. Barone and Miss N. Aprà in Milan, to Prof. F. Rossi in Florence, to Prof. A. Scrinzi in Brescia, and to Dr. R. Delbrueck in Bonn for their courtesies in obtaining suitable photographs, and to Miss Elizabeth Grundey for her help in the preparation of the manuscript.

CONTENTS

Historical Evidence

A VAST amount has been written about early Christian ivories seemingly out of all proportion to the limited number of objects belonging to this minor art.

Yet such interest is very natural. Few other works of art of this period have survived. Monumental sculpture had almost entirely died out, and, most important of all, Graeco-Roman pagan art had ceased to exist after giving birth to mediaeval Christian art.

This change was accomplished during a very troubled time. The vast organisation of the Roman Empire had collapsed, shaken by an unending series of political catastrophes prompted by all kinds of enemies. The Church, released from persecution and at last recognised by the State, had soon acquired great influence and power, but controversies and dogmatic disputes added religious motives to political ones in provoking war and disturbances.

The foundation of Constantinople and its rise as a great city shifted imperial power to the East ; soon the natural administrative division between East and West became a political one, growing more and more pronounced as a result of religious and cultural differences, and ultimately this led to complete rupture.

From a period so unstable in every way it would be unreasonable to expect an art homogeneous in style and with a definite form of evolution. And indeed many monuments surviving from this period, whether they be mural paintings, mosaics, illuminated manuscripts, carved stone sarcophagi or ivory reliefs, present problems that are often vital to our understanding of the development of mediaeval art, yet impossible to solve with our scanty knowledge of what was happening artistically in Alexandria, Rome, Milan and Arles, Antioch, Constantinople and Ravenna in these 4th-6th centuries.

1

Ivories, easily transportable, often copied in contemporary or later times, without sufficient intrinsic value to make them precious in periods indifferent to the beauty of their carving, emerge in our times after mysterious journeys through a tenebrous past.

Fortunately some of them carry a message which makes their origin clear, while others give a convincing enough indication of their approximate date and provenance.

Fig. 35 For example, precise information is found on some of the diptychs, especially consular diptychs. Of these there exist a fair number dating from the beginning of the 5th to the middle of the 6th century. Also a monogram carved on the front of the famous ivory bishop's throne in Ravenna indicates its first owner, the bishop Maximianus (545-556), and obviously limits the time of its manufacture to before 556. This helps to date other ivories closely related to it by style and iconography.

It became customary in the 4th century to commemorate important personal events by sending out *faire-part* tablets in the form of diptychs decorated on the outside with some appropriate subject, while the inside, hollowed and covered with a thin layer of wax, contained the message. When made of ivory, ink could have been used.

The diptychs were normally in wood, the most costly in ivory and gilt. The latter were considered of such ostentatious luxury that in 384 a law prohibited their used by anyone except the two consuls. They alone had the right to send "their names and portraits, engraved on gilt tablets of ivory, as presents to the provinces, the cities, the magistrates, the senate and the people." Of these, the most elaborate, sometimes so large that each leaf was assembled from five pieces of ivory, were destined for the emperor himself. The richness of the decoration on the others varied according to the importance of each recipient.

Figs. 19, 20, 44 In most of the diptychs, the consul is represented in front of the tribunal or presiding in the circus. Seated on the curule chair, dressed in his magnificent robes, he holds in his

2

right hand the *mappa circensis,* the kerchief to be thrown down as the signal for the start of the games. To complete the scene, there are usually carved in the lower part of the diptych chariot races, fights between men and animals, groups of actors, mimes, acrobats and dancers. Sometimes instead of Fig. 49 these animated scenes, there are two men pouring out money from sacks, in order to symbolise the generosity of the nominated magistrate.

As the name of the consul was used as the legal date of the year throughout the Empire, we have no difficulty in dating these reliefs except of course where the inscriptions have been subsequently mutilated by neglect or use.

By an unlucky coincidence, or perhaps for some reason yet unknown to us, the dated consular diptychs from the 5th century all belong to Roman consuls, while those from the 6th century were all given by consuls nominated in Constantinople. A diptych of Orestes (Rome, 530) is the only exception, but it imitates so closely the diptych of Clementinus (Constantinople, 513) that it ranges with the Eastern series.

It has been observed that the early Western group displays a great variety of styles. In most of these diptychs an attempt at portraiture has been made in the representation of the figures ; the lettering follows the style of the carving and was obviously made at the same time. There is little doubt that the diptychs were designed especially for the occasion. We can therefore state with some assurance that their dating corresponds with the time of their manufacture, and that they were commissioned in an atelier of ivory carvers situated within the geographical circle of the consul's activities. If the consul was nominated in Gaul, for instance, he could have ordered the diptychs to be made in Gaul, provided that ivory carvers were available there at that time and had adequate skill for such an important undertaking.

The later Eastern group is very different. The diptychs give the impression of being copied from a model composition. Throughout a comparatively long period, the style does not change much ; the faces lack individual character ; the names of the consuls are little more than scratched in the space provided for this purpose and do not show the same careful execution as the relief. From these observations we can assume that the diptychs may have been prepared in quantity beforehand, bare of any inscription, and engraved only at the moment of purchase. They give us, therefore, only an approximate indication of date and little indication of place of origin, which could as well be Constantinople as any other place within the Eastern Empire supplying the artistic market of the capital. Nevertheless the ivories represent the expression of official taste in Constantinople at that period because of the elevated position of their purchaser.

Although the two groups do not provide us with a much wanted example of two carvings made simultaneously in the two different centres of the Empire, we may assume that the common artistic language of the Hellenistic era had already split in the Mediterranean into several styles that were gradually drifting apart.

All these facts provide a scaffolding which, although incomplete and inadequate in many places, is solid enough for us to attempt to build a history of early Christian ivories.

Style and Iconography

The first Christians were poor, living in simplicity with a contempt for riches. Art was for them not only a visible sign of opulence but a form of idolatry repeated endlessly in sculpture and in painting, in every public place and in every rich private house. The early Church avoided art, when not dismissing it entirely.

The first known paintings are in the catacombs, and they do not seem much earlier than the end of the 2nd century. They look more like the zealous work of a decorator turned Christian, who wanted to offer his art to the divine cause, than a planned attempt at religious decoration.

The style, although it cannot be compared to some of the glorious murals of Pompeii, uses similar idioms. It is the illusionistic style from Alexandria, swift and effective, prompt to use effects of light and shade, able in catching a familiar gesture, arranging figures in casual groups against an attempt at realistic landscape and architecture.

It was natural that this art should reach the catacombs. It was the common artistic language of all countries around the Mediterranean Sea where Hellenistic culture had spread throughout a world that had been unified under the Roman rule to an extent never before or since achieved.

The Alexandrian style was not, however, the only expression of Hellenistic art. The retrospective attitude of Graeco-Roman culture was always ready to accept more or less sincere revivals of earlier periods. Returns to aesthetic ideas of the great 4th and 5th centuries B.C. were encouraged by sophisticated connoisseurs who collected early works either in original or in imitations. From such inspiration rose an artistic movement rightly called Neo-Attic because of its obvious ancestry.

Entirely academic and uncreative, the Neo-Attic style faithfully followed classical rules. In relief and painting,

5

figures were arranged symmetrically, singly or in groups against a plain background, usually presented in three-quarter view and composed so that their movements were determined by a single plane. Giving no illusion of space, each composition was self-sufficient, the action confined within the limited space of the frame.

Both aspects of Hellenistic representation were widely adopted in official Roman art. The cosmopolitanism of the Mediterranean world, and wide migrations of craftsmen, evenly distributed Hellenistic art throughout the Empire, and it would be difficult to trace the supremacy of one style over another at the time of its full expansion. Only at its decline, when the tide of Hellenistic culture ebbs, can we estimate from the patterns left by its waves that the Alexandrian style left a more durable impression on the Latin West, while the East was naturally inclined to follow the Neo-Attic trend.

At the same time we note the reappearance of pre-Hellenic traditions, especially in countries with an artistic past foreign to Greek aesthetics. In Mesopotamia and Persia the heritage of the ancient hieratic art had never been entirely forgotten, and now it again influenced the art of the whole near East. In Egypt, although Alexandria was still a stronghold of Hellenism, the Nile valley elaborated its own style. This Coptic Art, influenced equally by Hellenic and by Oriental sources, with a tendency to primitivism, expressed itself fluently in decorative art, and, which interests us especially, in an energetic school of ivory carvers.

With the spread of Christianity both the Asiatic hinterland and the Nile valley saw an ever increasing number of hermits. These soon gathered together in monasteries. Even in the humblest form of worship the elementary liturgical accessories achieved an artistic appearance owing to the zeal of the donor. With the growth of the monastic life, the Church became an insatiable recipient of the riches and beauty which the monks were so strictly denying themselves. When Constantine's uneasy conscience prompted him to bestow lavish donations upon the Church, they took the shape not only of gold for charities but also magnificent adornments for the altar and sumptuous vestments for the clergy. Books were written, copied and illustrated to make their contents more easily understood to the reader. The codex and not the roll became the popular form of the book, and had to be bound.

This sudden and extensive demand for art had to be supplied from the nearest artistic centre. It borrowed from every available source, rejecting the too obvious pagan imagery, readily adopting neutral ornament, and courageously improvising new Christian figural subjects for which there was no model.

The first simple symbols known to us from the catacombs were borrowed from pagan representation and symbolism : palms, peacocks, doves, flowering shrubs, vines and so on. The Hellenistic Helios or Orpheus became the youthful, beardless Christ. Hermes Criophorus served as a model for the Good Shepherd. This type of Christ later gave place to a more imposing vision, the hieratic Christ-the-God, bearded and severe. In the same way Christ the philosopher, seated amongst his followers and conversing amiably with them, later became the enthroned emperor of Byzantine art, surrounded by the Evangelists, Apostles and Saints, judging the living and the dead.

The first figural compositions to be entirely original were simple scenes from the Old and the New Testaments. The story of Jonah, Daniel amongst the lions, Moses striking the rock, Noak in the Ark, David, Job, Tobias and the Miracles of Christ were represented as reminders of litanies in which the infinite generosity of God was celebrated. Then single scenes became grouped in narrative series, following a formula known to Latin imagery and employed in such monumental works as the Trajan and Antonine columns as well as in reliefs decorating sarcophagi, with Christian subjects now imperceptibly replacing mythological figuration.

Alexandrian illusionism, or rather what was left of it at that time, was the medium best suited to telling a story in a serial form easily understandable by everyone. But the transcendental character of Christian teaching was more easily expressed in Neo-Attic representation, already greatly influenced by oriental hieratism.

Figs. 15, 17

Fig. 48

Sometimes two parallel versions of the same scene persist for a long period before one finally eliminates the other. The narrative version of the Adoration represents the Kings approaching the Virgin from one side, carrying gifts. The hieratic representation is entirely static, with the Virgin seated at the centre, frontal and indifferent to the scene ; and as there are two kings on one side of her and the third on the other, an angel is added to balance the composition.

Although condemned by the Church as being narratives based on doubtful if not entirely false tradition, apocryphal gospels provided the artists with many picturesque details for which they looked in vain in the New Testament. Many of the apocryphal texts, written at the same time as the first ivories were carved, indicate that their place of origin, or where they achieved popularity, was also the source of the ivories' iconography.

Through long tradition the Church has accepted for ever the vision of the artist, although based on the fantasy of a writer that was long ago condemned.

The Fourth and Fifth Centuries

The earliest known Christian ivory is probably the superb *Figs.* 1, 2 casket in Brescia. No other example can be compared to its consummate art, still faithful to Hellenistic tradition. The figures, in strict three-quarter view, are grouped in carefully balanced compositions, in which the studied arrangement sometimes even detracts from the clarity of the narrative. For instance, in the episode of Pilate washing his hands, Christ has been relegated to the far end of the composition —a flat unfolding of an overcrowded scene. This, together with the stilted appearance of the figures, accounts for the impression that the casket is by an imitator of great ability copying, without creative imagination, painted compositions in serial form, in a medium still faithful to a more monumental approach. This criticism can also be applied to other contemporary work in sculpture, especially to the carvings of the sarcophagi, where similar lack of spontaneity is apparent. The forms of Greek art had by now lost their noble proportions, and their features were being used awkwardly in an art still uncertain of its expression.

Although superior because of its admirable craftsmanship the casket finds its place easily in the series of monuments from the paintings in the catacombs to the wooden doors of St. Sabina in Rome.

It is much more difficult accurately to place the diptych *Fig.* 3 with Adam and St. Paul. Many details suggest that its origin is very close to that of the casket, but all the animals, in imitation of some oriental textile pattern, have been displayed in strict isolation all over the carved surface ; and even on the leaf with the episodes of St. Paul's life, where illusionism still seems to be prevalent, a frontal composition makes its appearance in the central scene.

Frontality is achieved throughout in a diptych in which, *Fig.* 4 we believe, the unhappy Stilicho, his wife Serena and son

Fig. 5
Eucherius are portrayed, and in another diptych, preserved at Novara, representing an unknown patrician. As the figures have an elegant elongation foreign to contemporary Latin work, we are inclined to see these carvings as first examples of a style invading North Italy from Constantinople, and which later on will be responsible for the long rows of frontally displayed figures in the colourful mosaics of Ravenna's churches.

There is a fair number of ivories from around 400 which can be confidently accepted as made in Rome. Most of them are diptychs.

From early times the survival of diptychs was assured by their liturgical use : it became customary to inscribe in their hollowed inside names of the living and the dead for whom prayers were asked during the mass. Many diptychs must have been made especially for this purpose and this accounts for the choice of subjects like Paradise, the Resurrection or the Ascension, but certainly consular as well as private diptychs were similarly used, although decorated with pagan imagery.

At that time some of the great Roman families, still faithful to ancient idolatry, were giving particular emphasis to their creed, and commemorative diptychs provided an excellent opportunity for such demonstrations. This attitude naturally coincided with a nostalgic revival of classicism. The famous
Fig. 6
diptych believed to have been made to commemorate a marriage between members of the Nicomachi and Symmachi families clearly shows both tendencies. It represents pagan rites and is carved in the manner of a Greek funeral monument many centuries older. The heavily mutilated Cluny part seems to be of happier composition than the Victoria and Albert leaf, where even academic imitation appears to be beyond the artistic power of the carver. The careful perfection of detail only underlines the poverty of the composition. The proportions of the lady resemble the shortened figures of many other ivories belonging to the same period.

The diptych of Probus on which the emperor Honorius is *Fig.* 9 twice represented obviously imitates official statuary. We pause to wonder whether the heavily shaped and flabby figure is an artisic convention already adopted, or an attempt to portray the inglorious ruler whose lazy life behind the safe walls of Ravenna coincided with the most tragic episodes in the decline of Rome.

In religious subjects, the carvers, deprived of models from antiquity and thus relieved from academic imitation, were discovering a new approach to their art. The beautiful leaf *Fig.* 7 of the Maries at the Sepulchre from Milan is still imbued with the Hellenistic spirit, but there is a new dramatic tension much deeper than the surface of the carving and already foreign to antiquity. The composition, apparently artificially divided by the frame in the middle, is in fact made more moving, for the two groups, psychologically and emotionally contrasted, have thus been clearly separated.

Below there is an admirable feeling of peace, adoration and entire fulfilment because of Jesus' Resurrection ; above, there are two poor terrified soldiers confronted by an extraordinary adventure beyond their understanding.

The problem of contrasting reactions to the same event as seen by those who knew the truth and those who were ignorant must have been of great concern to an early Christian artist still living in a half pagan, half Christian world. This also accounts for the poignancy of another ivory relief : the Ascension, from Munich. *Fig.* 10

The soldiers are asleep or indifferent. The three Maries are approaching with beautifully expressed respect, emotion and expectation. One of them repeats the gesture of Christ in the Arrestation scene and of St. Peter in the Denial on the Brescia casket—a gesture probably very expressive to the Romans, great viewers of pantomimes, but which has since lost all significance. But there is no difficulty in understanding the vividly described emotions of the two disciples overwhelmed by the majestic pace of the Ascension.

In the Adoration of the Magi the Western narrative had

become the fixed iconographic model. In the Ascension, however, the Western realistic representation of Christ walking upon clouds and lifted by the hand of God to Heaven has given way to the Eastern vision where Christ rises vertically supported by flying angels.

Fig. 12 Six scenes from the life of Christ, divided between Berlin and Paris, are the only fragments which survive from a composite book cover. The simplicity of each composition magnifies the clarity and directness of every movement and gesture. The completeness and brevity in the dramatic expression of every episode results in a monumental character very rarely achieved in ivory.

Though the mothers' desolation in the Massacre of the Innocents can be compared to some ancient Greek representation of grief, it would be impossible to find a parallel to the intense expression of compassion in Christ facing the distorted, tragic face of the demoniac, in the sad story of the Gadarene swine. The drama is not of this world, and that the artist was able to describe it in simple, human language is a precocious example of wide humanism in a form that developed fully only many centuries later.

There is a number of ivories which display similar iconographic themes and details of composition. In the style and treatment of the carving gradual changes can be observed, pointing to a school of ivory carvers which must have been active for a long period. It is difficult to imagine that Rome remained its centre all the time in spite of the political catastrophes of the 5th century. Probably repeated invasions and pillage dispersed many craftsmen, who travelled perhaps as far North as Trèves, and later came back to Arles, Milan and Rome when chances of peace and some prosperity were forthcoming. New arrivals of craftsmen from Egypt could explain the renewal of Alexandrian traditions, so vivid again *Fig.* 15 in scenes carved on the Werden casket.

Not only are episodes from the Virgin's life take from an apocryphal gospel probably written and certainly very popular in Egypt, but the personification of the river god is unmistakably Alexandrian. These carvings are closely related to the panels with Moses, St. Peter and St. Paul, and to the Fig. 16 beautifully preserved complete reliefs of a book cover from the cathedral in Milan. This last monument shows a long Fig. 17 narrative in numerous scenes treated with great mastery but it has already lost the poignant simplicity of the Berlin-Paris fragments. The wreath and ribbon ornamentation, the border motif and the angular treatment of the draperies suggest the style of the consular diptychs near the end of the century, although many beautiful details and a superior style prevent too close association with the returning primitivism of the Boethius diptych. Fig. 19

An invasion of artistic ideas from the Asiatic East accounts for some of the ivories made in the middle of the century.

For historical reasons Arles has been suggested as the place of manufacture of the Asturius diptych. The regular distri- Fig. 20 bution of carved elements all over the surface to achieve an even, decorative play of light and shade, and the frontality of isolated figures differing in size in proportion to their importance, may show a complete acceptance of oriental fashion or simply the presence of oriental craftsmen in Gaul or North Italy. Their chisels would also be responsible for the most controversial relief, with the Apotheosis of an Fig. 21 emperor, on which Latin pagan ideology is expressed in a strange attempt at hieratic symbolism. It is less surprising to find a monument of paganism in the middle of the 5th century than to encounter such a fanatical effort to assure the survival of idolatry by enriching it with a transcendental character imitated from Christianity.

It is impossible to disregard the unity of artistic expression which relates several ivories to the Apotheosis. To the similarity in the movement of the figures, the treatment of the hair, the shape of the " mushroom " trees and the engraved motifs which link one relief to another, must be added a more important link : the abandonment of illusionism and the adoption of an evenly ornamented surface, with a tendency to isolate the elements in the composition.

Fig. 22 This effect is entirely achieved in the Lion's Fight in which the extraordinary vitality of the men and animals is comparable to the best examples of Mesopotamian art. The *Fig.* 23 Bellerophon panel seems purely Eastern, with its horse-shoe architectural frieze, a motif difficult to find in the West. Asiatic and Alexandrian elements are equally mixed in the *Fig.* 24 Helios-Selene diptych, in which the portrait of nature, land and sea, is almost entirely composed of personifications. A Western, even a Roman, character is very present in the *Fig.* 25 diptych with the figures of Rome and Constantinople. The decorative elements, the symbolism and the "wet" draperies moulded to the bodies are still close to the style of the diptychs that imitate statuary from the beginning of the century. On the other hand, the hybrid style of the Rome-Constantinople diptych suggests an art transplanted artificially from a site with its own ancient tradition to a new place where all traditions join to produce a highly polished composite official art. And that means Constantinople.

The accidental way in which some examples have survived when so many have probably perished, is liable to mislead us by providing seemingly paradoxical results to our observations. In any case, the last examples only confirm the general picture of art in the 5th century as a melting pot in which varied artistic tendencies were mixed together. Yet already a new trend was emerging, or rather several new trends. It is their success or failure which makes the history of the following ten centuries of Mediaeval art, in the West as well as in the East.

The Sixth Century

In an attempt to show the elusive character of artistic evolution in ivory carving during the 5th century, we have assembled the most representative reliefs in groups united by a similarity of style.

All these groups can claim either a Western origin or at least some detail of iconography or ornamentation which links them with the West. Outside these groups we have purposely left a few isolated examples which, although obviously belonging to the 5th century, by their Eastern origin are more naturally linked to the ivories of the 6th century. Most of them are pyxes, and all seem to come from Egypt or the Near East.

Circular boxes are naturally suggested by the shape of an elephant's tusk cut into segments. Coptic art, sketchy and expedient, made great use of such shaped ivory pieces, both for decorating furniture and for the manufacture of boxes. Greek artists, residents of Alexandria, followed their example, and boxes with continuous figural compositions on their curved sides must have been an important item in the Egyptian ivory trade.

The Church soon adopted ivory boxes as receptacles for the Eucharist. To be so used they were appropriately decorated with sacred subjects. None the less boxes with profane and even decidedly mythological subjects were made as late as the 6th century. And not only were these used without scandalising anybody but some of the boxes so decorated found their way into churches and thus secured their preservation to our times.

In contrast to the accidental mythological imagery adorning many pyxes, the figure of Orpheus carved on the beautiful box from Bobbio is, we may guess, an allusion to *Fig.* 26 Christ. In spirit, the decoration is close to similar representations from the catacombs, yet the beasts surrounding the inspired harpist are here displayed in a way already far from familiar illusionism : figures are isolated and the deep under-cutting only emphasises the artist's preoccupation with the even distribution of a pattern made from light and shade all over the surface of the object.

Fig. 27 In the panels of Poets and Muses the artist shows the same interest in a rhythmical arrangement of forms displayed regularly against a flat background. Deep carving insures contrasting play of light and shade, making the isolation of the figures more pronounced. They are imbued with a certain nostalgic air of Hellenistic tradition, mysteriously preserved in the folds of their light draperies, but the figures themselves are petrified in a novel arrangement. Movements which could have been fluent and natural against an Alexandrian landscape here appear as if suddenly interrupted, and we marvel at the extraordinary balance of the Muses, keeping awkward poses in perfect immobility.

The same preoccupation with an even distribution of accents all over the carved surface can be observed on the *Fig.* 28 Berlin pyx, although the effect is achieved in a different manner. Here the figures are not isolated. On the contrary, they are very close, often even coming in front of each other, and their forcible gesticulation cleverly fills any remaining space. The Hellenistic tradition, still followed in a superficial illusionism, is breaking up in the search for a new, more abstract, attitude to art. Christ is represented as a philosopher talking to his pupils, and the scene leads without any interruption to the Sacrifice of Abraham. There is no other connection between the two episodes than Eucharistic symbolism. The message is beyond the realistic representation of the actual scenes and the dramatic gestures of Christ's disciples are as accidental as the harmonious repose of the Abraham group. The artist is no longer interested in realistic detail nor in the right psychological expression. He admits the complete failure of his illusionistic art in trying to represent trans-cendental beliefs, and naturally gravitates to hieratism.

The stilted Neo-Attic and the decadent remains of official

16

Roman art at the beginning of the 6th century were more easily adapted to this attitude and Constantinople certainly encouraged an art well suited to the pompous ostentation of its court.

The large panel with an Archangel from an imperial *Fig.* 29 diptych seems to be an important instance of this official art. There is a tradition of excellent craftsmanship in the carving and realism in the detail. None the less the carver disregarded logical representation in his work. Accumulated conventions of possibly Byzantine fashion in the diptychs of Stilicho and the unknown Patrician erupt here and cause a complete lack of co-ordination between the human figure and its surroundings.

Standing awkwardly across a flight of steps situated inside an arch supported by two columns appears the Archangel with arms and wings illogically projected in front of the columns. We " accept the gift " of this magnificent piece of carving with all its fine detail and decorative appeal, but we would like to " learn the cause " of its lack of nobility and style.

Neither nobility nor style is lacking in the short figure of *Fig.* 31 the Empress which we think may also have been made in Constantinople. Here the evolution of hieratic monumentality is accomplished. The figure is human and abstract at the same time. There is an expression of transcendental power which Byzantine art later invokes at will in all divine representations.

The consular diptychs here again give information about the artistic taste of the capital although this time it is Constantinople. There is no doubt that with the 6th century, parallel to advanced hieratic conceptions there was another strong artistic current of a different character. It is not very difficult to recognise the Egyptian idiom, although it had changed from the Alexandrian style which influenced the West some centuries before. Originating in Egypt, it was chiefly, it seems, wherever it was made, intended for the Byzantine market.

17

It is an art more interested in decorative values than in the expression of philosophical ideas. Its narrative style is vivid and imaginative but deprived of psychological insight. It amuses rather than moves. It ranges from really Coptic sensuality and coarseness to an exquisite vivacity and precision in noting a picturesque detail or in following the rhythm of a sensitive line.

Fig. 30   On one side there is a relief with Apollo and Daphne. The artist takes a sceptical attitude, not deprived of humour and obvious sensuality, towards a too well known mythological subject. And a similar spirit animates the vivacious scenes *Fig.* 32 from a Bacchic cycle.

On the other side there is the genuine loveliness of the *Fig.* 33 Ariadne from the Louvre and the refined grace of the two victories (or are they already angels ?) holding a wreath with the bust of Constantinople, in one of the two fragments preserved at Milan from an imperial diptych. The other fragment, in spite of its beautiful and highly polished carving, is tiresome because of its too pedantic symmetry. There is the same subject treated on the corresponding part of the *Fig.* 43 Barberini imperial diptych, in which the group of barbarians bring their offering in a more expressive composition of extraordinary rhythm and fluency.

The same quality of bold and expressive carving is mani-*Figs.* 44, 46 fested in the picturesque scenes from the theatre or hippodrome when they appear on contemporary consular diptychs. The figure of the consul himself with all his attributes is usually presented in a dry hieratic manner.

Another example of the extremes to be found in this art of *Fig.* 34 such uneven styles is the panel from Trieste. It shows such vulgarisation of Hellenic themes that we hardly recognise Castor and Pollux, Europa and the bull, and Zeus, in a naively inserted medallion above the scene. The awkward use of conventional ornament and the caricatural approach to human figures place this carving on the border of popular art. We can certainly assume that it was Coptic art which produced this decadent piece.

But the same contrast of figural compositions alternating with ornamental scrolls as well as conch shells is used with great virtuosity in the complex panelling of the most important work of the school—the magnificent throne of bishop Maximianus at Ravenna.

Figs.
35—42

It has been observed that the chair is the work of at least two different hands. Some writers have even suggested that it was assembled from parts made in different places and during a period of time of some length, the front panel with the Latin monogram of Maximianus being added as a final piece in Ravenna, while the main body of the chair was made in the East, a theory to which Greek assembly marks seem to bear witness.

Without going into far-reaching speculation, it is easy to detect the difference in style between the deeply carved front panels, closely related to the more shallow reliefs with scenes from the life of the Virgin and Christ and the Joseph cycle, treated again in a higher relief. Nevertheless, still more striking is the consistency of artistic attitude throughout a work of such complexity.

We can admire the nobility of the figures of St. John and the four evangelists, reminiscent of classical greatness, but at the same time we have to deplore the contemptible disregard for the same nobility in proportions that change according to the wider or narrower space allocated to each figure and its architectural frame. The human form is treated here in the same way as decorative ornament, the proportions and riches of whose vegetal and animal motifs are entirely determined by the available space.

The panels illustrating the New Testament and its apocryphal additions are composed in a spirit of real devotion which is expressed by a softer line and a truly lyrical approach to the subject. The Joseph scenes are more dynamic in general, and more anecdotic in detail. Nevertheless there is everywhere the same decorative apprehension of the void and the architectural accents are used rather to complete the narrative and enrich the surface than to give an illusion of space. The shallow and deep carving can be explained by practical reasons if not by a decorative need for contrast, as in the case of the difference between the central panel and the borders of the Barberini diptych.

On the throne as well as on the imperial diptych reminiscences of Graeco-Roman pagan conventions are still present in spite of the changed general artistic attitude, caused by the complete adoption of a new religious imagery—often stabilised in a definite form. The personification of Earth appears under the feet of the Emperor's horse, and victories are still present as symbols, having abdicated their right to divinity. Christ is baptised in the river Jordan, which still appears as a mythological person with or without upturned jar. And when Christ enters Jerusalem He is acclaimed not only by a joyful populace but also by the City herself holding a cornucopia.

Figs. 45, 50 Whole subjects and many of the details represented on the throne are repeated in other monuments of ivory, mostly on book covers which seem to have become very popular carved in ivory by that time. They are often composed of five elements in the same way as the large imperial diptychs. And the similarity is not limited to the construction.

There is the same motif of angels, and here they are definitely angels, holding a wreath with the cross. The place of the emperor is taken by the figure of Christ or the Virgin, seated in majesty and surrounded by evangelists, saints, angels or, in the case of the Lady, adoring Kings. The side and bottom panels are divided into familiar scenes from the life of the Virgin, of the miracles of Christ, and, in one instance of a book cover but again repeated on pyxes surprisingly reminiscent of old Alexandrian representation, there is the cycle of Jonah.

Jonah cast away from the ship into the sea, and Jonah naked and resting under the gourd tree, are represented with picturesque volubility and an illusion of space entirely absent in other scenes on the book cover. In these, figures dissociate themselves from the usual grouping and turn towards us in isolation and frontality. At the same time, in scenes of a more complex narrative character, they become fragmentary and are treated with a brevity alarmingly near to primitivism. This is very marked in the Adoration of the Kings and the Nativity from the other leaf of the book cover from Murano. The limbs have reached a stage further from the smooth, sensual, rondity, very Coptic, which we observed in the Ariadne and the Apollo and Daphne. They have become dry, stiff and angular. And this, in spite of the picturesque detail, and decorative variety of forms and texture, is very apparent in the panels from Aix-la-Chapelle. *Fig. 47*

In 541 we lose the guidance of the consular diptychs, the consulate having been abolished by Justinian.

In the last example of the series, the diptych of Justinius, a *Fig. 49* very important detail of iconography makes its first dated appearance : Christ is bearded and with a cruciform nimbus. He is represented in the same way in the arch of the basilica, high above a ceremonial procession, in a rather enigmatic panel from Trèves, unlike any other ivory carving from the *Fig. 51* period.

Although the figures in high relief resemble the figure of the Empress from Florence, as well as similar representations on consular diptychs, the mixture of an extraordinary realism with the tendency to organise the whole scene into long rows of figures naturally suggests a link, across the dark age of iconoclasm, between the art of Constantinople in the 6th century and the great Byzantine Renaissance of the 10th century.

In the Murano book cover, in spite of all the difference of style which dissociates it from the throne, Christ is still represented as a young man, beardless and curly haired. Each time He appears on the panels of the throne, He is represented in a similar way. A medallion with His effigy inserted in the border surmounting the back of the throne is almost identical with the medallion on the Barberini diptych.

And again He is portrayed in a similar way wherever He appears on the book cover of Echtmiadzin. But on a book

21

Fig. 50 cover of the same style in the Bibliothèque Nationale, a very strange iconographic dichotomy is taking place. In narrative scenes treated with a vivacity not very distant from the best examples of the school, Christ preserves His youthful appearance, but in the central panel, seated on the throne, hieratic, He has a long pointed beard and a cruciform nimbus. And this representation finally eliminates the other in subsequent examples of ivory of similar style and design, all displaying strange mannerism in affixing ears on the temples, and a degenerate technique of carving in a more and more pronounced way.

Again as with the examples of the 5th century, there is reason to deplore the chance that determined which ivories should survive. We have not enough material to be able to decide which change of style is the result of distance in time and which of distance in space, especially at the time when consular diptychs disappeared for good, and illustrated manuscripts, always the inspiration of the ivory carver, are not numerous enough to enlighten us.

Some of the new trends which appeared in the previous century seem to have vanished entirely. But it is only an eclipse and they reappear in Carolingian art which conserved and developed this precious heritage of our Western civilisation.

BIBLIOGRAPHY

DALTON, O. M.   *Catalogue of the Ivory Carvings of the Christian Era in the British Museum.* 1909.

DALTON, O. M.   *Byzantine Art and Archeology.* 1911.

LONGHURST, M. H.   Victoria and Albert Museum. *Catalogue of Carvings in Ivory.* Part I. 1927.

DELBRUECK, R.   *Die Consulardiptychen und verwandte Denkmäler.* 1929.

KOLLWITZ, J.   *Die Lipsanothek zu Brescia.* 1933.

PEIRCE, H., ET TYLER, R.   *L' Art Byzantin.* 1932-1934.

KITZINGER, E.   *Early Medieval Art in the British Museum.* 1940.

MOREY, C. R.   *Early Christian Art.* 1942.

CECCHELLI, C.   *La cattedra di Massimiano ed altri avori romano-orientali.* 1936-1944.

DE LOOS-DIETZ, E. P.   *Vroeg-christelijke ivoren.* 1947.

VOLBACH, W. F.   *Elfenbeinarbeiten der Spätantike und des frühen Mittelalters.* 1952.

CECCHELLI, C.   *Vita di Roma nel Medioevo. I. Arti minori e il costume. Fasc. 4: Avori.* 1951-1952.

23

DESCRIPTIVE NOTES TO PLATES

Measurements are given in inches and millimetres.

1—2. CASKET, known as Lipsanotheca of Brescia. SCENES FROM THE NEW AND THE OLD TESTAMENTS. The large compositions on the lid and central bands of the four sides represent scenes from the New Testament: on the lid, Christ in Gethsemane, the Arrest of Christ, St. Peter's denial, Christ before Caiaphas, and Christ before Pilate ; on the right side, the Healing of the blind, and the Raising of Lazarus ; on the back, the Transfiguration, and the Punishment of Ananias and Sapphira ; on the left side, the Raising of Jairus' daughter ; on the front, the Healing of the woman with issue, Christ amongst the doctors, and the Good Shepherd. Compositions with smaller figures represent scenes from the Old Testament : on the left side, Moses on Mount Sinai, the destruction of Korah and his companions, Moses receiving the law, Jacob and Rachel at the well, Jacob wrestling with the Angel, and Jacob's ladder ; on the back, an " orant " woman (Susanna ?), Jonah under the gourd vine, Daniel and the serpent, the Finding of Moses, Moses slaying the Egyptian, and the scene with a festive meal, the meaning of which is not clear ; on the left side, David and Goliath, the Man of God slain by the lion and watched by the ass, the Idolatry of Jeroboam, and the Worship of the golden calf ; on the front, two scenes from the story of Jonah, Susanna and the elders, Susanna accused, and Daniel and the lions. Along the four sides of the lid, Christ (in the centre of the front side), the four evangelists and the twelve apostles (?). On the lid, above the figural compositions, doves caught in a net (salvation of the souls) ; on the four corners, various symbolical figurations—a tree, a funeral monument and a balance, a tower, Judas hanged, the cross, a lamp, a fish, a cock on a column. The casket is the earliest known Christian sculptural monument on which a cyclical method of narrative has been attempted. H.9⅝(245). L.13½(317). W.8⅝(220). Brescia, Civico Museo Cristiano. North Italy, about 360-380.

3. DIPTYCH : ADAM IN PARADISE. The composition of Adam surrounded by animals is inspired by some antique representation of Orpheus ; the four rivers of Paradise are symbols of the four Gospels. SCENES FROM THE LIFE OF ST. PAUL. St. Paul preaching and St. Paul at Malta : the kindling of the fire, the viper fastened on the hand of the saint, the miraculous healing of the Roman officer's father and others with various diseases. H.11¾(295). W.(of each leaf) 5¼(135). Florence, Bargello. North Italy (?), about 380-400.

4. DIPTYCH : STILICHO, HIS WIFE SERENA AND SON EUCHERIUS. The diptych was probably made to commemorate the nomination of Eucherius as tribunus and notarius in 395.

Stilicho was consul in 400.   H.12¾(322).   W.6⅜(162).   Monza, Cathedral.   North Italy, probably Milan, about 395.

5.   DIPTYCH : UNKNOWN PATRICIAN.   The style suggests the art of Ravenna. H.13¾(330). W. (of each leaf) 5½(141). Novara, Cathedral.   North Italy, probably Ravenna, about 400-425.

6. DIPTYCH, bearing the name of the SYMMACHI and NICOMACHI. The diptych was probably made to celebrate a marriage uniting the two great Roman families in 392-3. The subject—young women performing a service in the temple—and style, inspired by Hellenistic models, were purposely chosen to emphasize the paganism to which the families were faithful. The harmonious composition of the Paris leaf suggest a close copy from a Greek original. The London leaf, in contrast, appears clumsy, being an academic imitation of a style already beyond the artistic powers of the carver.   H.11⅝(295).   W. (of each leaf) 4¾(120). L. leaf : Paris, Cluny. R. leaf : London, Victorian and Albert Museum.   Rome, about 390-400.

7. LEAF OF A DIPTYCH : THE MARIES AT THE SEPULCHRE. The convention of *three* Maries in this scene has not yet been established. As a result of the conventional perspective, which places foreground figures below instead of in front of the more distant ones, the soldiers have accidentally been relegated to the roof of the monument. Above them are the symbols of two evangelists ; the symbols of the other two presumably appeared on the lost second leaf of the diptych. On the doors of the tomb are familiar scenes of the life of Christ: the Raising of Lazarus, Zacchæus on the tree, and a miracle of Christ of which only a fragment can be seen. H.12⅛(310).   W.5¼(134).   Milan, Castello Sforzesco.   Italy (Rome ?), about 400.

8. DIPTYCH OF PROBIANUS, VICAR OF ROME. Nothing is known of this official. In a similar way as in fig. 7, a decorative border divides figures in the foreground from the remaining figures. H.12¾ and 11¼ (316 and 300). W. (of each leaf) 5(129). Berlin, Staatsbibliothek.   Rome, about 400.

9. CONSULAR DIPTYCH OF PROBUS. The Emperor Honorius is represented on both leaves. Except for the Constantine monogram of Christ surmounting the labarum, the composition simulates traditional Roman statuary, including all the conventions of pose and dress, the nimbus around the head, and a victory standing on an orb. The precocious obesity of the Emperor, who was then about 22, and the expression of the face (in which a likeness was certainly attempted), seem to confirm the cowardly and lazy character of the man known from texts.   H.11¾(299).   W. (of each leaf) 5⅛(131). Aosta, Cathedral.   Rome, 406.

10.   PANEL: THE ASCENSION AND THE MARIES AT THE

SEPULCHRE. The canon of *three* Holy Women visiting the Tomb is adopted. Christ lifted up by the hand of God, and the figures of the two disciples dazzled by the supernatural light coming from above, are full of movement and vigour. The architecture of the building, with its pretentious accumulation of ornament, appears out of date amongst figures designed with such simplicity and boldness. The birds on the tree symbolize eternal life. H.7⅜(187). W.4½(116). Munich, National Museum. Italy, about 400-425.

11. LEAF OF A DIPTYCH, bearing the name of the LAMPADI. A dignitary with two attendants is presiding in the hippodrome at a chariot race. Similar to contemporary Christian carvings, this ivory has the same quality of power and concentrated life. H.11⅜(290). W.4¼(110). Brescia, Civico Museo Cristiano. Italy (Rome ?), about 400-425.

12. PANELS from a composite diptych or book cover : SCENES OF THE LIFE OF CHRIST. The Massacre of the Innocents, the Baptism, the Miracle at Cana, the Healing of the woman with the issue, the Gadarene swine and the Healing of the paralytic. Unless one thinks about Giotto and Masaccio, it is difficult to find equal greatness expressed so simply and directly. Each scene brings its emotional content to a climax. The artist entirely eliminated all unnecessary detail, and is concerned only with the human figure and its movement. He was able to capture a whole range of expression in the four attitudes of Christ in the miracle scenes : the peaceful concentration at Cana, the arrested movement with the imploring woman, the compassionate sadness when facing the demoniac, and the decisive gesture when giving an order to the paralytic. There is also all the difference between the despair of the lamenting mothers and the tragic face of a madman. L. panel : H.7⅞(200). W.3⅛(81). Berlin, Kaiser Friedrich Museum. R. panel : H.7¾(197). W.3(78). Paris, Louvre. Italy, about 420-430.

13. PANELS FROM A CASKET : SCENES OF THE PASSION. Pilate washing his hands, Christ bearing the cross, and the Denial of St. Peter ; Judas hanged and the Crucifixion ; the Maries at the Sepulchre ; the Incredulity of St. Thomas. By comparison with other examples from this group, the composition seems to suffer from an excessive concern with naturalism. Though the Maries are relegated behind the soldiers and the scene has lost its dramatic effect, some of the figures have acquired extreme vitality : Pilate, St. Peter and Longinus piercing Christ's side. The representation of the Crucifixion is of extreme rarity at such an early period, and this is probably the earliest in existence. H.3(75). W.3⅞(98). London, British Museum. Italy, about 420-430.

14. LID OF A CASKET : A MUSE AND POETS. In spite of the shortened proportions of the bodies, there is a harmony in the composition which is more the result of the robust directness of the new Christian art than of a still very live Hellenistic tradition.

H.4¾(120). W.6¾(170). Paris, Bibliothèque de l'Arsenal. Italy, about 420-430.

15. PANELS from a casket, known as the Werden Casket : SCENES FROM THE LIFE OF THE VIRGIN AND CHRIST. The Annunciation at the spring, St. Joseph's dream, the Visitation, the Virgin entering the temple for the trial of the bitter water ; the Magi seeing the star, the Nativity, the Adoration of the Magi ; St. John the Baptist preaching, " the Axe laid to the root of the tree," the Baptism. Most of the scenes are inspired from apocryphal gospels. The Hellenistic river-god makes an imposing appearance in the Baptism. Not only the decorative motif used in the border, but also the attitude of the figures, remind us of the Probus diptych. II.1¾(45). L.6(155) and 10(255). London, Victoria and Albert Museum. Italy, about 425-450.

16. PANELS from a casket. MOSES striking the rock; ST. PETER raising Tabitha ; ST. PAUL and Thekla, and the Stoning of St. Paul. H.1¾(42). W. 3⅜(98). London, British Museum. Italy, about 425-450.

17. GOSPEL-BOOK COVER: SCENES FROM THE LIFE OF THE VIRGIN AND CHRIST. In the upper corners are symbols of the four evangelists above their respective effigies in the lower corners. Between these are the Nativity, the Adoration of the Magi, the Massacre of the Innocents, and the Miracle at Cana. In the centre of the leaves are the Agnus Dei and a cross in metalwork, flanked by the Annunciation by the spring, the Magi seeing the star, the Baptism, the Virgin entering the temple for the trial of the bitter water, Jesus amongst the doctors, the Entry into Jerusalem, the Healing of the blind, the Healing of the paralytic, the Raising of Lazarus, a scene of difficult interpretation which resembles the multiplication of the loaves in other examples, the Last supper, and the Widow's mite. H.14¾(375). W. (of each leaf) 11(281). Milan, Cathedral. Italy, about 450-480.

18. DETAIL of Fig. 17.

19. CONSULAR DIPTYCH OF BOETHIUS, consul in 487. There is a marked lowering in the skill of the carver, who is unable to achieve any convincing interpretation of the human body, and attempts at a " cubist " simplification of the draperies, a mannerism that had already made a noticeable appearance in the Gospel-book cover (figs. 17-18). H.13¾(350). W. (of each leaf) 5(126). Brescia, Civico Museo Cristiano. Italy (Rome?), 487.

20. LEAF OF A CONSULAR DIPTYCH OF ASTURIUS, consul in 449. The primitivism of the composition can be easily explained as provincial work, but the leaf is also an example of western art

27

strongly influenced by eastern ideas. H.6¾(172). W.5(127). Darmstadt, Landesmuseum. Italy or Gaul, 449.

21. LEAF OF A DIPTYCH: APOTHEOSIS (CONSECRATIO) OF AN EMPEROR. The panel represents the funeral of an emperor. Four elephants carry the effigy of the emperor under a canopy. His deified figure rises from the funeral pile on a chariot drawn by horses accompanied by two eagles. Still higher, winged figures carry the emperor to heaven, represented by a portion of the zodiac, an assembly of gods, and the sun. The monogram on the frame is probably standing for SYMMACHORUM. It has been suggested that the diptych was dedicated to Antoninus Pius on the 300th anniversary of his funeral (463). It has also been suggested that the represented emperor is Julian the Apostate (d. 363). The piling up of pagan symbolism appears as a late attempt to create pagan iconography as opposed to Christian. H.10⅞(277). W.4½ (113). London, British Museum. Rome, about 430-460.

22. DIPTYCH : LION FIGHT. An admirable display of vigour and boldness in the carving of the men and beasts. Accentuated by the isolation of the figures, the composition has a strong eastern flavour. The movement of some of the figures is identical with some in fig. 21, and generally there is great similarity in many details. H.12¾(322). W. (of each leaf) 4⅞(125). Leningrad, Ermitage. Rome (?), 430-460.

23. LEAF OF A DIPTYCH : BELLEROPHON. The subject of Bellerophon's fight with the Chimera was very popular in the late classical period. Too many details link this ivory with those of figs. 21, 22 and 24 to suggest an eastern provenance only on the account of the horseshoe arcade. Arches of similar style appear on fig. 16. The cutting away of the background seems rather a mutilation made in some later period than the initial intention of the carver of this beautiful ivory. There is no other instance of an open-work panel in ivory at that time, and it would be difficult to explain its purpose. H.8⅜(212). W.3½(88). London, British Museum. Italy, about 430-460.

24. DIPTYCH : WINE AND OIL HARVEST, known as HELIOS AND SELENE. The exuberant display of gods and goddesses assisting at the wine and oil harvest does not seem to witness to a revival of paganism similar to that in the Apotheosis, but rather, in imitation of Alexandrian style, they are assembled as personifications of all the elements of a complex sea and landscape. H.12½(315), W. (of each leaf) 5(126). Sens, Cathedral. Italy, about 420-450.

25. DIPTYCH : ROME AND CONSTANTINOPLE. In many consular diptychs, the consul is accompanied by personifications of Rome and Constantinople. Here they occupy the whole of this diptych. It has been suggested, from the victory held by Rome and

the cupid perched on the shoulder of Constantinople, that the diptych was made to commemorate a marriage uniting families from the two cities. A beautiful example of late Roman official art inspired by Alexandria. H.10¾(274). W. (of each leaf) 4½(115). Wien, Kunsthistorisches Museum. Italy (Rome ?), 420-450.

26. PYX : ORPHEUS PLAYING TO BEASTS. Around the central figure of the musician, a whole antique menagerie, including centaurs, winged lions, satyrs, and other supernatural animals, is gathered. The reality of such fauna being generally accepted, there is nothing irreverent in its surrounding Orpheus, if he symbolizes Christ. H.6¼(160). Bobbio, Abbay of S. Colombano. East Mediterranean (Egypt?), about 400.

27. PANELS : POETS AND THEIR MUSES. In a similar way as in fig. 28, the figures are displayed like a textile pattern, all over the carved surface. The declining skill of the carver breaks up into jerky movements what might have been a harmonious dance if it had been represented by a Hellenistic artist a few generations before. H.11½(290). W. (each panel) 3(75). Paris, Louvre. East Mediterranean, about 400-450.

28. PYX : CHRIST SURROUNDED BY HIS DISCIPLES. SACRIFICE OF ABRAHAM. Christ is represented as a philosopher disputing with his pupils. The carver obviously copied the Sacrifice of Abraham from some image which he could not entirely understand, and therefore the pile of wood and the altar built by Abraham have become an elaborate building. H.4¾(120). D.5¾(146). Berlin, Kaiser Friedrich Museum. East Mediterranean, about 400.

29. LEAF OF A DIPTYCH : ARCHANGEL MICHAEL. At the top of the leaf there is an inscription in Greek " Receive these gifts, and having learned the cause . . ." It has been suggested that the diptych was offered to the emperor of the East in reconciliation in 518. H.16⅞(428). W.5⅝(140). London, British Museum. Constantinople, about 518.

30. PANEL : APOLLO AND DAPHNE. Apollo holding a lyre and accompanied by a swan and cupid approaches Daphne, who is already changing into a tree. Under Coptic influence, what degenerate Alexandrian art loses in elegance it gains in energy. Expressive and often sensual crudity is the Egyptian counterpart to western simplicity, resulting from concentration on spiritual problems. H.4⅞(124). W.3½(87). Ravenna, National Museum. Egypt, about 450-500.

31. PANEL: AN EMPRESS. This is probably the central panel of an imperial diptych. The Empress represented is probably Ariadne (d. 515), daughter of Leon I., who married in turn Zenon

and Anastasius. Embroidered on her cape is thus the portrait of her son Leon, consul in 473. The mystical majesty of the empress is already as distant from the superficial nobility of Roman official art as from the simplicity of early Christian humanism. In this example we clearly see the character of Byzantine art, five centuries before its apogee. Such a hieratic portrait of an empress easily served as a model for the representation of the Virgin in Majesty. H.12(305). W.5⅜(136). Florence, Bargello. Constantinople, about 500.

32. PANELS from a casket: BACCHIC SCENES. The accurate and witty observation of an Alexandrian artist gives liveliness to four scenes representing Bacchus's fight with the Indians, who refused the introduction of the vineyard to their country. The prisoner taken into captivity in the lowest compartment is held in a similar way to Joseph in fig. 39. H.5⅛(150). W.3½(90). St. Gallen, Stiftsbibliothek. East Mediterranean (Egypt?), about 500-550.

33. ARIADNE. A very rare instance of carving almost entirely in the round, and a beautiful example of late Alexandrian art at its best. The main figure of the girl is traditionally believed to be Ariadne, the love of Bacchus, here poetically surrounded by nature swarming with supernatural life. H.12½(420). W.5½(138). Paris, Musée de Cluny. East Mediterranean (Alexandria ?), about 480-500.

34. PANEL: CASTOR AND POLLUX, THE RAPE OF EUROPA. A return to primitivism, bringing this panel close to an example of popular art, does not entirely explain an obvious caricature of mythological themes. H.8(202). W.5¼(134). Trieste, Museo Civico. Egypt, about 550-600.

35. BISHOP'S CHAIR, known as Cathedra of Maximianus. This is certainly the most important object in ivory preserved from the early Christian period, and also one of the most beautiful. Despite its modest size, as opposed to its elaborate and profuse decoration, the chair has a monumental character entirely due to its fine proportions. The boldness of the carving, the extraordinary liveliness of the figures and the fluency of decorative motives, give an impression of improvisation only underlined by a complete disregard for any precision in the tracing of straight lines or right angles. The carving is of great skill and beauty, and, as differences of style suggest at least two different artists working on the figural compositions, it is certainly a work of an important atelier of ivory carvers with an established tradition. On the front of the chair, St. John the Baptist and the four evangelists under the monogram of Maximianus, bishop of Ravenna (546-556). At the back of the seat, surmounted by Christ in a medallion, scenes from the life of the Virgin and Christ, continued at the back of the chair ; of the twenty-four original panels, eleven are missing. On the sides, ten panels with episodes from the story of Joseph. H.47(1190). W.24½(620). Ravenna, Arcivescovado. Alexandria (and Ravenna ?), about 520-550.

36. BISHOP'S CHAIR, detail: ST. JOHN THE BAPTIST AND THE FOUR EVANGELISTS. St. John the Baptist is easily identifiable by the Agnus Dei and the fur cape. H.19⅛(487). W.20⅞(530).

37. BISHOP'S CHAIR, detail: THE BAPTISM. Christ is represented as a boy standing in the river with the traditional river-god holding an upturned jar. THE ENTRY INTO JERUSALEM. Christ is welcomed by the personification of the city of Jerusalem ; behind, on a tree, is Zacchæus, carved with realism smaller than the other figures. Each panel: H.10¼(260). W.4¾(120).

38. BISHOP'S CHAIR, detail: THE ANNUNCIATION. The angel appears to the Virgin while she is weaving the veil of the temple, as described in apocryphal gospels. The angel, contrary to a later established iconographical canon, stands to the right of the Virgin. H.8¼(210). W.4½(113).

39. BISHOP'S CHAIR, detail: THE STORY OF JOSEPH. IV. Joseph is sold to Potiphar, represented in two episodes: Joseph carried on a camel, and the actual moment of the sale. Behind Potiphar are standing his wife and a servant. V. Joseph tempted by Potiphar's wife and Joseph cast into prison, where are the king's butler and baker. H.14(357). W.7¼(185).

40. BISHOP'S CHAIR, detail: THE STORY OF JOSEPH. III. The sorrow of Jacob at the sight of the " coat of many colours " ; space is indicated by the architectural motif in perspective and by the figure of Benjamin standing on the second plane. I. Joseph is cast into the pit ; above his head is a star ; to the left, the brothers are dipping Joseph's coat in the blood of a kid ; in the background, a palm suggests the countryside ; the two scenes, symmetrically balanced, are accompanied by the figure of Reuben three times repeated, expressing his anxiety, discontent and despair. II. Joseph is sold to the Ishmaelites. H.13¾(351). W.10¼(260).

41. BISHOP'S CHAIR, detail: THE STORY OF JOSEPH. VIII. Joseph receives his brothers ; the soldiers are dressed like the barbarians represented on Roman monuments ; one of the soldiers holds Simon as a hostage ; the three brothers wear the pastoral attire of shepherds. IX. The distribution of corn ; the carver, for reasons of clarity, has given the corn the size of a banana ; Joseph supervises the work, seated on a throne. VII. Joseph expounds dreams to the Pharaoh; the Pharaoh is seated on a throne; behind him stand soldiers; behind Joseph are two official interpreters of dreams. H.14(357). W.10½(265).

42. BISHOP'S CHAIR, detail: THE STORY OF JOSEPH. X. Joseph receives his father and brothers ; to the left, Egyptian soldiers express their amazement. VI. The Pharaoh's dream; in front of the Pharaoh asleep on his bed stands the winged figure of Hypnos (Sleep). H.9⅞(251). W.7½(190).

43. LEAF OF AN IMPERIAL CONSULAR DIPTYCH, known as the Barberini diptych. In the upper part: Christ in a medallion held by angels. In the centre: the emperor (Anastasius ?) on horseback. Victory is personified to the right. The earth brings fruits to the emperor's feet, and a defeated enemy (Bulgarian ?) stands behind the horse. To the left, the consul presents a victory. Below, a group of barbarians are bringing their tribute under the guidance of yet another victory, in a composition of beautifully varied and balanced figures and movements. H.13½(341). W.10½(266). Paris, Louvre. East Mediterranean (Egypt?), about 500-520.

44. CONSULAR DIPTYCH OF ANASTASIUS, consul at Constantinople in 517. The consul is seated on a curule chair, holding a sceptre and the *mappa circensis*. The heads in the two medallions surmounting the chair on either side are of the Emperor Anastasius and his wife Ariadne. They are probably also represented, together with the traditional figures of Rome and Constantinople, in other medallions on the chair, sceptre, etc. Below, scenes from the circus, introducing a lively note to the pompous and conventional arrangement of the diptych. H.14⅛(360). W. (of each leaf) 5⅛(130). Paris, Bibliothèque Nationale. East Mediterranean (Constantinople ?), 517.

45. LEAF OF A BOOK COVER, known as the Murano diptych. In the upper part, on each side of angels holding the cross in a wreath, stands an archangel with cross and orb. In the centre is Christ with St. Peter and St. Paul and two angels. Below are the Three children of Babylon in the furnace. On the sides are the Healing of the blind and of the demoniac, the Raising of Lazarus, and the Healing of the paralytic. In the lower part are two episodes from the story of Jonah. H.14(355). W.12(305). Ravenna, National Museum. East Mediterranean (Constantinople ?), about 510-530.

46. CONSULAR DIPTYCH OF ANASTASIUS, details: Amazons, comic and tragic actors ; scenes from the circus.

47. RELIEF: A HORSEMAN. One of a set of six reliefs remaining from a throne decoration. The horseman resembles in pose and in dress the emperor in the Barberini diptych (fig. 43) and was obviously inspired by that or a similar composition. Victorious in a fight with some dangerous animal, crowned by victories or angels, he is, perhaps, representing a holy knight—prototype of St. George. H.9⅝(245). W.4⅞(125). Aachen, Cathedral. East Mediterranean (Egypt?), about 530-570. *(Photo. from* Carlo Cecchelli *La Cattedra di Massimiano.)*

48. PANEL: THE ADORATION OF THE MAGI. THE NATIVITY. The Kings approach from both sides to give a symmetrical aspect to the scene. An angel has been added to complete the balance, the apocryphal number of three kings already being an iconographic canon. Below: a Nativity scene in which the figure of St. Joseph is omitted but the unbelieving midwife, Salome, is introduced, raising her withered hand towards the Child. H.8½(215). W.3⅜(85). London, British Museum. East Mediterranean, about 520-560.

49. CONSULAR DIPTYCH OF JUSTINIUS, consul at Constantinople in 540. This diptych is the last of the series, the consulate being abolished in 541. At the same time, it is the first dated monument on which Christ is represented bearded and with a cruciform nimbus. He is represented on both leaves between Justinian and Theodora. The bust of Justinian terminates the sceptre held by the consul. The little men pouring out money symbolize the generosity of the consul. H.13¼(335). W.5⅛(130). Berlin, Kaiser Friedrich Museum. Constantinople, 540.

50. GOSPEL-BOOK COVER, known as the St. Lupicinus Gospel-book. SCENES FROM THE LIFE OF THE VIRGIN AND CHRIST. Both leaves have at the top a similar panel of angels holding a wreath with a cross. In the central panel of each there are, respectively, Christ between St. Peter and St. Paul and the Virgin and Child with two angels. These are flanked by four miracles of Christ (the Healing of the blind, the paralytic, the woman with issue, and the demoniac) and four scenes from the life of the Virgin (the Annunciation, the Visitation, the Trial by bitter water, and the Journey to Bethlehem). In the lower panels: Christ and the Samaritan woman, the Raising of Lazarus, and the Entry into Jerusalem. In all the scenes, Christ is represented as a young beardless man without nimbus, except in the central panel where He is bearded and with a cruciform nimbus. The style is very close to the bishop's throne at Ravenna ; some of the scenes are similarly composed and even the mannerism of ears placed high on the temples is present, but the carving is much looser, there is rather hastiness than boldness. H.16⅛(405). W.12⅝(320). Paris, Bibliothèque Nationale. Egypt or Gaul (?), about 550-600.

51. PANEL: TRANSPORTATION OF RELICS. In a street of a town (Constantinople ?) there is a procession in which the emperor and the empress are taking part. In a chariot is a bishop, with an assistant, holding the casket containing the relics. Above, under an arch, appears Christ bearded and with a cruciform nimbus. The rows of people are set within the architectural divisions of the buildings, similarly to the rows of saints appearing so often in later Byzantine ivories. H.5⅛(131). W.10¼(261). Trier, Cathedral. Constantinople, about 540. (Photo. from Richard Delbrueck Die Consular Diptychen.)

ACKNOWLEDGEMENTS

The writer wishes to thank the following for permission to reproduce photographs: Alinari (3, 5, 9, 19, 30, 31, 34, 35, 40, 41, 42, 45), Anderson (36, 37), Archivio Fotografico, Brescia (1), British Museum (13, 16, 21, 23, 29, 48), Giraudon (4, 6a, 10, 12, 14, 22, 27, 28, 33, 43, 44, 46, 50), Istituto di archeologia cristiana, Rome (47), Kunsthistorische Museums, Wien (25), Foto Paoletti di Mario Zacchetti (7, 17), Rühl, Darmstadt (20), Gust. Schwarz, Berlin (8, 49), Victoria and Albert Museum (6b, 15), Dr. George Zarnecki (2).

Printed by Suttons, Paignton.

1. CASKET: SCENES FROM THE NEW AND OLD TESTAMENTS.
About 360-380

2. CASKET: SCENES FROM THE NEW AND OLD TESTAMENTS
About 360-380

3. ADAM IN PARADISE. SCENES FROM THE LIFE OF ST. PAUL
About 380-400

4. STILICHO, SERENA

CHERIUS. *About* 395

5. Unknown Patric[

6. Diptych. *About* 390-400

7. The Maries at the Sepulchre. *About* 400

8. PROBIANUS, VICAR OF ROME. *About* 400

INNOMINE
XPI·VINCAS
SEMPER·
DN·HONORIO·SEMP·AVG
DN·HONORIO·SEMPER·AVG
ROBVS·FAMVLVS·V·C·CONS·ORD·
PROBVS·FAMVLVS·V·C·CONS·ORD·

9. Consular Diptych of Probus. 406

10. The Ascension and the Maries at the Sepulchre.
About 400-425

11. Leaf of a Diptych. *About* 400-425

12. Scenes of the Lif

ST.   *About* 420-430

13. Scenes of the Passion. *About* 420-430

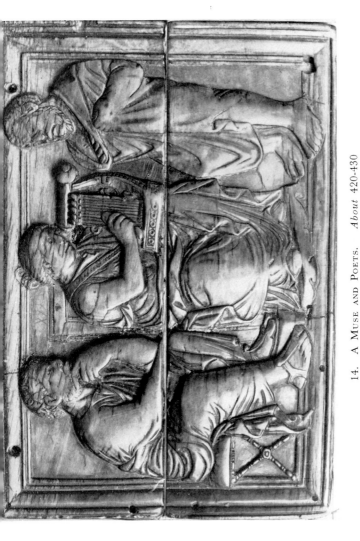

14. A MUSE AND POETS. *About* 420-430

15. Panels from a Casket. *About* 425-450

16. PANELS FROM A CASKET. *About* 425-450

17. GOSPEL-BOOK CO

bout 460-480

18. *Detail of figure 17*

19. Consular Diptych of Boethius. 487

20. Leaf of a Consular Diptych of Asturius. 449

21. APOTHEOSIS OF AN EMPEROR.   *About* 430-460

22. Lion Fight. *About* 430-460

23. BELLEROPHON. *About* 430-460

24. Wine and Oil Harvest. *About* 420-450

25. ROME AND CONSTANTINOPLE. *About* 420-450

26. PYX: ORPHEUS PLAYING TO BEASTS.   *About* 400

27.　Poets and their Muses.　*About* 400-450

28. PYX: CHRIST AND HIS DISCIPLES.   THE SACRIFICE OF
ABRAHAM.   *About* 400

29. ARCHANGEL MICHAEL. *About* 518

30. APOLLO AND DAPHNE. *About* 450-500

31. AN EMPRESS. *About* 500

32. BACCHIC SCENES. *About* 500-550

33. ARIADNE. *About* 480-500

34. CASTOR AND POLLUX. THE RAPE OF EUROPA. *About* 550-600

35. Bishop's Chair. *About* 520-550

36. Bishop's Chair *detail*: St. John the Baptist and the Four Evangelists

37. Bishop's Chair *detail*: The Baptism, the Entry into Jerusalem

38. Bishop's Chair *detail:* The Annunciation

39. BISHOP'S CHAIR *detail*: THE STORY OF JOSEPH (IV. AND V.)

40. Bishop's Chair *detail*: The Story of Joseph (III., I. and II.)

41. BISHOP'S CHAIR *detail*: THE STORY OF JOSEPH (VIII., IX. AND VII)

42.   Bishop's Chair *detail*: The Story of Joseph (X. and VI.)

43.　Leaf of an Imperial Consular Diptych.　*About* 500-520

44. Consular Diptych of Anastasius. 517

45. Leaf of a Book Cover. *About* 510-530

46. *Details of figures 44*

47. A HORSEMAN. *About* 530-570

48. THE ADORATION OF THE MAGI AND THE NATIVITY.
About 520-560

49. Consular Diptych of Justinius. 540

50. Gospel-Book Cover: Scenes from

. OF THE VIRGIN AND CHRIST.   *About* 550-600

51. TRANSPORTATION OF RELICS.   *About* 540